This Journal belongs to

____

Made in the USA
Las Vegas, NV
22 September 2021

30879102R00069